Who Was
Julius Caesar?

D0036831

Who Was
Julius Caesar?

By Nico Medina
Illustrated by Tim Foley

Grosset & Dunlap
An Imprint of Penguin Group (USA) LLC

To my parents, for introducing the Medina kids
to the Eternal City—NM

GROSSET & DUNLAP
Published by the Penguin Group
Penguin Group (USA) LLC, 375 Hudson Street, New York, New York 10014, USA

USA | Canada | UK | Ireland | Australia | New Zealand | India | South Africa | China

penguin.com
A Penguin Random House Company

Library of Congress Cataloging-in-Publication Data is available.

ISBN 978-0-448-48083-1   10 9 8 7 6 5 4 3 2 1

Contents

Who Was
Julius Caesar?

More than two thousand years ago, a twenty-five-year-old man from Rome was traveling by boat to the Greek island of Rhodes. He was going to study public speaking there.

Suddenly, another ship appeared—a ship full of pirates! They were from Cilicia—what is now southern Turkey. Cilician pirates were feared throughout the ancient world. They were known to hijack large trading ships, steal the cargo, and sell the passengers into slavery.

But these pirates were not interested in making a slave of the young man from Rome. He was too important for that. He came from a famous family and was known for his bravery in battle. The Romans would pay a high ransom for his return.

The young man knew this. So when the pirates were set to demand twenty talents for his freedom, he laughed in their faces. A man of his fame was surely worth *fifty* talents. (That would be more than $30 million in today's money!)

Messengers were sent ashore with the pirates' ransom demand, while back aboard the pirate ship, the young man did not act worried at all. He joined in the pirates' exercises and games. If the pirates were too loud when he wanted to sleep, he sent his servant to tell them to quiet down. Sometimes, he made his captors listen to him recite poems and speeches he had written. If they acted bored, he called them stupid and threatened to have them killed the first chance he got. The pirates thought, *What a joke!* What could one prisoner do to a whole gang of pirates?

After more than a month, the ransom finally arrived. The young man was set free. As soon as he got back on dry land, he raised a fleet of warships and returned to punish the pirates.

The pirate ship was right where it had been. With little trouble, he captured the entire group and imprisoned them in a nearby Roman town. But was this enough to satisfy the young man's desire for revenge? No. He took each and every one of the pirates and had them killed.

No one messed with this man known as Julius Caesar. Those who did, lived to regret it . . . if they were lucky enough escape with their lives.

Over his lifetime, Julius Caesar doubled the size of the Roman Republic. He ruled over it single-handedly as "dictator for life," the first man to do so in nearly five hundred years.

Julius Caesar changed Rome, and the world, forever.

Chapter 1
Young Caesar

Julius Caesar was born in Rome in the year
100 BC. As a boy, he was tall and slender, with a
full, round face, dark hair, and intense black eyes.

Julius Caesar was named after his father. His
mother's name was Aurelia, and his two older
sisters were both named Julia. That was probably
very confusing!

His family lived in Subura, a poor neighborhood of crowded apartment buildings. Many former slaves and foreigners lived there. Caesar's family was not rich or powerful, but they were *patricians*. This meant they were Romans of "noble" blood. They traced their roots back hundreds of years. Caesar's family said they were descended directly from Venus, Roman goddess of love and beauty!

No one in Caesar's family had done anything very important in many years. As his parents' only son, much was expected of young Caesar.

His father taught him to fight with the Roman warrior's weapons of choice: a long spear, a short sword, and a shield. Caesar learned to swim in the Tiber River and to ride horses on the Field of Mars. He wasn't the biggest or strongest boy, but Caesar worked hard. He was such a good horseman, he could ride with his arms behind his back—without a saddle!

At home, Caesar learned basic reading, writing, and math skills from his mother and a private tutor—a slave from Greece.

RELIGION IN ANCIENT ROME

THE ROMANS BORROWED A LOT FROM THE CULTURE OF ANCIENT GREECE. THEY COPIED GREEK ARCHITECTURE; GREEK WAS ONE OF THE REPUBLIC'S TWO OFFICIAL LANGUAGES; AND THEY WORSHIPPED GREEK GODS—AFTER GIVING THEM ROMAN NAMES. THE MOST POWERFUL GREEK GOD, ZEUS, BECAME THE ROMAN GOD JUPITER. THE GREEK GOD OF WAR, ARES, WAS RENAMED MARS. POSEIDON, THE GREEK RULER OF THE SEAS, WAS NEPTUNE TO THE ROMANS. A GOD OR GODDESS EXISTED FOR ALMOST EVERYTHING—THERE WAS EVEN A GOD FOR MILDEW!

RELIGION WAS PART OF EVERYDAY LIFE IN ROME. ALMOST EVERYONE HAD A HOUSEHOLD SHRINE: A SMALL CUPBOARD WITH PICTURES AND TRINKETS WHERE THEY COULD PRAY AND MAKE OFFERINGS—OFTEN FOOD OR DRINK—TO THE GODS. IN TEMPLES, ANIMALS WERE SOMETIMES SACRIFICED TO PLEASE THE GODS. THE ROMANS BELIEVED IF THEY WERE GOOD AND GENEROUS TO THEIR GODS, THE GODS WOULD RETURN THE FAVOR.

When Caesar grew older, he learned Greek.
He also read and wrote poetry, and perfected his
skill at *oratory*—speaking before crowds. Being a
good orator was extremely important for anyone
who wanted to be a leader. If you could speak
powerfully, people could be persuaded to vote for
the causes you believed in.

EDUCATION IN ANCIENT ROME

IF BOYS DID NOT HAVE A PRIVATE TUTOR, THEY WENT TO SCHOOL. CLASSES STARTED BEFORE SUNRISE AND MIGHT BE HELD IN THE TEACHER'S HOME OR IN THE CITY STREETS AND PUBLIC SQUARES.

NOT MANY GIRLS WENT TO SCHOOL. AND BECAUSE SCHOOL WAS NOT FREE, NOT ALL ROMAN BOYS WENT TO SCHOOL. POOR PEOPLE COULD NOT AFFORD IT.

AT TEN OR TWELVE, MOST BOYS WOULD LEARN A TRADE. OTHERS, LIKE CAESAR, CONTINUED THEIR EDUCATION.

When he was a young man, Caesar went
to observe the Roman Senate debate, vote on
laws, and go about the business of running the
Republic. Years later, Caesar would give his own
speeches to the Senate. But for now, he simply
watched.

THE ROMAN REPUBLIC

IN CAESAR'S TIME, THE ROMAN REPUBLIC
STRETCHED FROM SPAIN TO MODERN-DAY TURKEY.
ROME WAS ITS CAPITAL CITY.

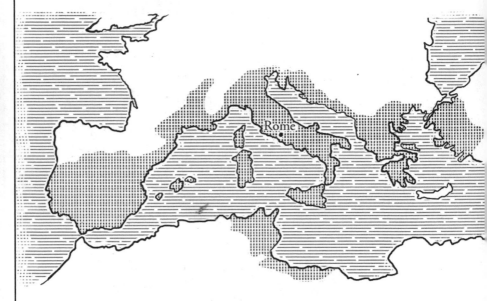

Rome

IN LATIN, THE WORD *REPUBLIC* MEANS "STATE
OF THE PEOPLE." FOUR HUNDRED YEARS BEFORE
CAESAR WAS BORN, THE PEOPLE OF ROME
OVERTHREW A POWER-HUNGRY KING. THEY
CREATED A REPUBLIC, WHICH WAS MADE UP OF THE
POPULAR ASSEMBLY AND THE SENATE, AND LED BY
TWO *CONSULS*.

THE TWO CONSULS WERE THE MOST POWERFUL
MEN IN ROME. BUT THEY COULD HOLD THE OFFICE

FOR ONLY ONE YEAR AT A TIME, AND THEY HAD TO SHARE POWER EQUALLY. WITH THESE LIMITS, NO INDIVIDUAL MAN COULD BE IN TOTAL CONTROL.

THE SENATE WAS FULL OF VERY WEALTHY MEN. SENATORS WERE APPOINTED TO THEIR POSITIONS BY THE CONSULS RATHER THAN ELECTED. THEY CREATED LAWS, ADVISED THE CONSULS, AND CHOSE MEN TO FILL GOVERNMENT POSITIONS.

THE POPULAR ASSEMBLY WAS MADE UP OF ALL CITIZENS OF ROME. THEY MET TO CREATE LAWS, DECLARE WAR AND PEACE, RULE ON PUBLIC TRIALS, AND VOTE FOR CONSULS. THE ASSEMBLY COULD ALSO STRIKE DOWN LAWS MADE BY THE SENATE AND REJECT THEIR GOVERNMENT APPOINTMENTS. ANY CITIZEN OF THE ROMAN REPUBLIC COULD VOTE IN THE ASSEMBLY. BUT ONLY MEN COULD BE CITIZENS, AND THE ASSEMBLY ONLY MET IN THE CITY OF ROME.

Chapter 2
Rome Divided

In the Republic, only two groups of people were allowed to vote: citizens of Rome and the lucky few outside Rome who were granted citizenship. They had to travel all the way to the capital to cast a vote. Most people in other cities held very little power.

When Caesar was nine, the cities surrounding Rome rebelled and went to war.

The Roman Senate chose Caesar's uncle Marius to put down the rebellion.

MARIUS

Romans loved Marius. His armies had once saved the city from an invasion. Marius was born a poor man, but he had risen to power. He was elected one of the consuls *seven times*! When Caesar's aunt (who was named Julia, just like his two sisters) and Marius wed, the family felt renewed pride. Their family name might once again be connected to greatness.

Marius, however, was unable to put down the rebellion. So the wealthy men of the Senate picked a new general to lead the troops. They chose a man with piercing gray eyes named Sulla. He was not as popular as Marius was

SULLA

with the people of Rome. But he put down the rebellion.

Now Sulla was promoted to lead armies in the east, where war was breaking out in another corner of the Republic.

Sulla's promotion made Marius very unhappy. Marius wanted to be the top general. *He* was the man the Romans adored—especially the poorer citizens of Rome. Sulla fought only to please the wealthy men in the Senate.

Rome became a city divided—some behind Sulla, some behind Marius. Sulla wanted to make the Senate more powerful. Marius wanted more power for the Popular Assembly and for Rome's poorer citizens. His troops, however, were no match for Sulla and his army, when they returned to Rome. Sulla's army burned down buildings and killed many people. Sulla was a Roman general. A Roman army had *never* marched on Rome!

There was nothing Marius could do but flee the city. Sulla traveled east again with his troops.

But Marius was not ready to give up the fight. He teamed up with a man named Cinna. They returned to Rome with their own army and began killing Sulla's supporters. Some victims had their heads chopped off and stuck to the ends of spears. They were displayed in the Forum for all of Rome to see.

Marius and Cinna became consuls together. Now they ruled the city.

THE ROMAN FORUM

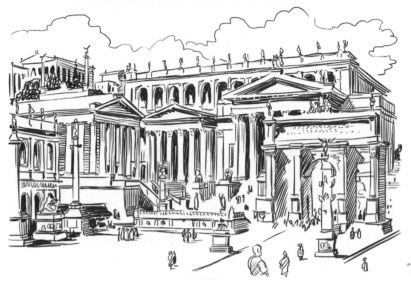

IN ANCIENT TIMES, ROME WAS THE BIGGEST CITY IN THE WORLD. AS MANY AS ONE MILLION PEOPLE WERE CRAMMED WITHIN ITS WALLS. IN THE CITY CENTER, THE OPEN SQUARES AND PROMENADES OF THE FORUM GAVE PEOPLE A CHANCE TO GET OUT OF THEIR CROWDED APARTMENTS AND STRETCH THEIR LEGS. THEY COULD SHOP FOR LUXURY GOODS FROM AROUND THE WORLD, VISIT PUBLIC BATHS, OR PRAY AT TEMPLES, MAKING OFFERINGS TO THE GODS. THE FORUM WAS THE BEATING HEART OF THE CITY, WHERE POLITICIANS CONDUCTED BUSINESS, NEW LAWS WERE POSTED, AND TRIALS WERE HELD.

Chapter 3
Picking a Side

Caesar had grown up in Subura, not in the hills above the city, where the wealthy lived. He understood why his poor neighbors were frustrated with the Senate: The rich didn't understand or care about their problems. When Marius died, Caesar sided with Cinna.

Around this time, Caesar's father also died suddenly. Now, at sixteen, Caesar was head of the household. He needed a job.

Cinna appointed him to become *flamen dialis* (FLAY-men dee-AL-iss), the High Priest of Jupiter. The god Jupiter was the protector of Rome. Being the god's High Priest was an important job indeed. Caesar had to marry a girl of noble birth. So Cinna arranged for him

CORNELIA

to marry his daughter, Cornelia.

As *flamen dialis*, Caesar's hair had to be cut with a bronze knife. No other kind was acceptable. Then the hair had to be buried. Caesar also wore a pointy hat made of fur.

And the feet of his bed had to be covered in mud. There were more rules, three of which really upset Caesar. He was forbidden from riding horses. He couldn't be a soldier, and he couldn't leave the city for more than three nights at a time. Caesar needed more than a fur hat to bring honor to his family.

It was a difficult time for a man to make a name for himself in Rome.

Cinna had grown mad with power. Wealthy citizens were being murdered by angry mobs.

Word came that Sulla and his forces were returning to Rome, and Cinna led his troops to meet the enemy. Cinna's troops realized they were no match for Sulla's army. So what did they do? They murdered their own commander.

But Cinna's death wasn't enough to satisfy Sulla. Once more, Sulla marched on Rome. For the third time in six years, the city was ablaze with Romans fighting Romans.

In troubled times such as these, the Senate sometimes elected one consul instead of two. This man was called a *dictator*, and he held all the power. They hadn't elected a dictator in nearly one hundred years. But now they did. Sulla won the job easily.

Sulla had always sided with the rich. He immediately extended the powers of the Senate and limited those of the Popular Assembly. He began clearing the city of his enemies. A list of names was posted in the Forum. Anyone who killed a man on the list could keep some of that man's property. (The rest went to the government.) Thousands were murdered.

Naturally, Julius Caesar was on Sulla's list. After all, he was Marius's nephew and had married Cinna's daughter. Sulla ordered Caesar to divorce his wife immediately. When Caesar refused, Sulla became furious. *No one* told the dictator no! Sulla stripped Caesar of his job and his money.

Fearing for his life, nineteen-year-old Caesar escaped to the mountains outside Rome.

With Sulla's men hot on his trail, he changed locations every night. Back in Rome, his family pleaded for his life. Eventually, Sulla relented.

Caesar was happy to come home, but he knew at any moment his life could be at risk again. So he became a soldier and left Rome. He would not return for years.

Chapter 4
Man of the People

Caesar's first post was in Asia, in what is now western Turkey. He was assistant to the Roman governor. Before Rome had conquered the area, it had been ruled by a king named Mithridates (mih-thrih-DAH-teez).

Some of Mithridates's allies were holed up on an island, refusing to surrender to Rome. Caesar's boss needed ships—and *quickly*!—to reach the island and wipe out the enemy.

Caesar got the ships

MITHRIDATES

from a nearby kingdom, and the battle was on!

He fought with such bravery, he was awarded the *corona civica*, or civic crown. It was a simple wreath made of oak leaves. Soldiers were given the crown for risking their own life to save someone. When someone wearing the civic crown walked into a room, everyone—even powerful senators—stood to show their respect. Caesar was making a name for himself.

Yet to rise to higher office and win honor for his family, Caesar knew he had to find a way to grab the public's attention and hold it.

When news of Sulla's death in Rome reached Caesar, he must have been overjoyed. It had been two years—now Caesar could return to Rome and enter politics!

He decided to become an advocate, which was a lot like being a lawyer. There was no such thing as a law degree in those times. Any educated man could act as an advocate. Trials were held at the Forum, and many people showed up to watch.

The better the advocate spoke, the more dramatic the trial, the bigger the crowd.

The first case Caesar took was for a group of people from the Roman province of Macedonia. They had traveled all the way to Rome to seek justice from their former governor. The Macedonians claimed he had profited from money they'd paid in Roman taxes. This happened all the time in Rome's provinces. But the Macedonians still wanted their day in court.

Being a good advocate wasn't just about what you said, it was also about how you said it. And Caesar's speech for the Macedonians was brilliant. He spoke passionately and vividly and really turned on the charm. Someone at the trial said that listening to Caesar speak was like seeing a portrait painted with words.

Nearly everyone in the Forum that day was impressed with Caesar. But the jury was made up entirely of wealthy senators. They ruled in favor of

the former governor, not the Macedonians. Caesar had lost the trial. Nevertheless, he was doing what he'd set out to do: Romans were not going to forget his name. He had a new reputation as a masterful advocate for the "little people." This would serve him well in the future.

Chapter 5
On the Rise

Not long after the trial, Caesar and Cornelia welcomed their first daughter to the world—and guess what Caesar named her. Julia!

Soon, Caesar was on the move again. If he wanted the good life for his wife and daughter,

he had to become an even *better* orator and soldier. So he set off for the Greek island of Rhodes to study with the great philosophers and orators of the day. It was on this journey that he was kidnapped by pirates.

But back in Asia, the rebel forces of King Mithridates were causing trouble again. So Caesar had to abandon his plans for Rhodes. Instead, Caesar rushed to help the Roman governor in Asia.

In Caesar's judgment, the governor was not acting strong enough. So what did Caesar do? He took over the army and led them into battle himself, defeating the rebels.

This was against the law. The *governor* was supposed to call the shots in his province. But Caesar didn't care. He'd do anything to bring glory to his family and to Rome. No one at home would ever cheer his name if he sat back and played by the rules.

SPARTACUS

A SLAVE NAMED SPARTACUS STARTED A WAR IN SOUTHERN ITALY. HE HAD BEEN CAPTURED BY ROMANS, AND HIS OWNER TRAINED HIM TO BE A GLADIATOR. GLADIATORS WERE MEN WHO FOUGHT WILD ANIMALS, OR OTHER MEN, TO THE DEATH IN FRONT OF A PUBLIC AUDIENCE FOR SPORT.

ONE NIGHT, SPARTACUS ESCAPED WITH MORE THAN SEVENTY OTHER SLAVES. THEY WERE ARMED ONLY WITH KITCHEN KNIVES. AS THEY FLED, THEY CAME ACROSS WAGONS LOADED WITH WEAPONS. SPARTACUS AND HIS MEN ARMED THEMSELVES AND HID IN THE MOUNTAINS. HERE, SPARTACUS RAISED A HUGE ARMY—TENS OF THOUSANDS OF MEN. THEY HELD OFF THE ROMANS FOR YEARS.

NO ONE KNOWS FOR SURE IF CAESAR FOUGHT TO SUBDUE THIS SLAVE REBELLION, BUT IT'S LIKELY THAT HE DID. IN THE END, SPARTACUS WAS KILLED ON THE BATTLEFIELD, AND THE REBELLION WAS ENDED. FOR DARING TO RISE UP AGAINST ROME, SIX THOUSAND REBELS WERE CRUCIFIED. THE CROSSES STOOD ONE EVERY HUNDRED FEET FOR A HUNDRED MILES, ALL ALONG THE ROAD TO ROME.

Caesar, now twenty-seven years old, received word from Rome. He'd been elected to public office! It was time to return home, once again.

Caesar was elected *pontifex*. He was now an even more important priest than he'd been before. It was another step up the Roman ladder of success. Luckily, the rules for being a pontifex were not so strict, and Caesar could remain a soldier!

A couple years later, Caesar was elected to another post, as *quaestor* (KWEH-ster). This was a government official who did any number of things for the Republic. There was a quaestor in charge of Rome's water supply, for example.

Caesar was probably thrilled to be assigned a post in faraway Spain. He had seen the eastern reaches of the Republic when he was a soldier in Asia. Now, as an important representative of Rome, he would journey west, to the edge of the known world.

Just as he was preparing to leave, tragedy struck
when Caesar's wife died. The two had known
each other since they were teenagers. Caesar was
brokenhearted. However, it did not stop him.
Shortly after the funeral, he went to Spain.

THE ROMAN WATER SYSTEM

ABOUT TWO HUNDRED YEARS BEFORE CAESAR'S BIRTH, ROME WAS ALREADY AN ANCIENT CITY EXPERIENCING GROWING PAINS. THE POPULATION WAS INCREASING, AND WATER WAS IN SHORT SUPPLY. COLLECTING IT FROM THE POLLUTED TIBER RIVER WAS NO LONGER SAFE. TO FIX THIS, ROMAN ENGINEERS LOOKED TO NATURAL SPRINGS HIGH IN THE HILLS OUTSIDE THE CITY. THEY DUG A TEN-MILE-LONG TUNNEL—THE AQUA APPIA, ROME'S FIRST *AQUEDUCT*—TO BRING THE FRESH WATER DOWNHILL INTO THE CITY.

MORE AQUEDUCTS WERE BUILT BEFORE CAESAR'S
TIME AND MANY MORE LONG AFTER HIS DEATH.
ONE WAS OVER FIFTY MILES LONG, AND SOME
STILL EXIST TODAY!

THE AQUEDUCTS FED PUBLIC FOUNTAINS AND
ROME'S GRAND PUBLIC BATHHOUSES. ROMANS
RICH AND POOR LOVED THE BATHS, AND THEY
VISITED AT LEAST ONCE A DAY. THEY TOOK GREAT
PRIDE IN THEIR CLEANLINESS, BELIEVING THE
BATHS WERE WHAT SEPARATED CIVILIZED ROMANS
FROM THE REST OF THE WORLD.

Caesar met with locals and listened to their problems, acting as a judge to settle disputes and gaining a reputation as a fair man. He returned to Rome by land, so he could stop in northern Italy. In this area, the people yearned for Roman citizenship, in order to enjoy the many rights that came with it. Caesar said he would do what he could to help. He was making friends and allies all over the Republic now.

Caesar could find political opportunity almost anywhere. Just before Cornelia had died, his beloved aunt Julia passed away. Caesar arranged her funeral and gave a speech honoring her. Rome's ruling class still considered Aunt Julia's husband (Caesar's uncle Marius) to be a bloodthirsty murderer. So it would have been smart for Caesar to keep the funeral private and quiet. But of course, Caesar had other ideas.

The funeral was held at the Forum. Caesar knew that most Romans still loved Marius. So Caesar led a long parade of people carrying large paintings of his aunt and his uncle.

Displaying pictures of Marius had been banned by Sulla fifteen years before. Now, veterans of Marius's armies wept openly at seeing his face after so many years.

Caesar gave a powerful speech as much about his ancestors as it was about Aunt Julia.

He told the crowd: "The family of my aunt Julia
is descended from kings on her mother's side and,
through her father, from the gods themselves. . . .
My family therefore holds the sanctity of kings
who rule among men and of gods who rule
over kings."

THE KNOWN WORLD

IF YOU LOOKED AT A MAP OF THE WORLD FROM CAESAR'S TIME, IT WOULD LOOK VERY DIFFERENT FROM THE WORLD WE KNOW TODAY. GREAT BRITAIN WAS SO FAR FROM ROME THAT MANY DIDN'T BELIEVE IT EXISTED. BEYOND GERMANY, MUCH OF EUROPE WAS UNEXPLORED. THE ATLANTIC OCEAN WAS BELIEVED TO BE THE EDGE OF THE WORLD (CHRISTOPHER COLUMBUS WOULD NOT CROSS IT FOR ANOTHER 1,500 YEARS!), AND WHAT LAY BEYOND

Dacia

Parthia

Mauretania

Egypt

Kush

THE SAHARAN DESERT IN AFRICA WAS A MYSTERY. TO THE EAST, ROMANS TRADED WITH THE CHINESE EMPIRE—A LAND THEY CALLED SERICA, WHICH MEANS "OF SILK" IN LATIN. BUT NO ROMAN WOULD VISIT CHINA FOR ANOTHER 200 YEARS. TRADE BETWEEN THE TWO EMPIRES WAS ARRANGED THROUGH MERCHANTS IN PARTHIA (MODERN-DAY IRAN).

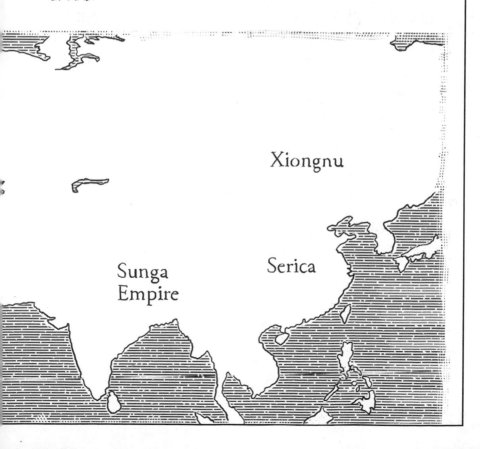

This was a smart way for Caesar to remind people of his noble background. Now, when they thought of Caesar, they'd think of kings and gods, and of Marius, beloved savior of Rome. That day, chants of "Caesar!" and "Marius!" echoed through Rome.

After his post in Spain, Caesar held a number of jobs in Rome. One was organizing public festivals and games. Here was another opportunity for Caesar to make his name known among the Romans. He borrowed tons of money to create lavish spectacles.

For one event, Caesar brought together more than six hundred of the Republic's best gladiators. Memories of Spartacus's rebellion were still fresh. Some feared that Caesar was trying to start another rebellion. But Caesar had other plans. He dressed the gladiators in pure silver. The crowds were dazzled as the sun reflected off so much shiny armor. Julius Caesar could really put on a show!

ALEXANDER THE GREAT

ALEXANDER THE GREAT WAS BORN TWO AND A HALF CENTURIES BEFORE CAESAR, IN MACEDONIA.

IN HIS SHORT LIFE, HE CONQUERED LANDS FROM GREECE TO INDIA. IN EGYPT, HE BUILT A GRAND CAPITAL FOR HIS EMPIRE AND NAMED IT ALEXANDRIA.

WHILE LIVING IN SPAIN, CAESAR VISITED A STATUE OF ALEXANDER THE GREAT ON AN ISLAND IN THE ATLANTIC OCEAN. CAESAR LOOKED UPON THE STATUE OF THIS MAN FACING OUT INTO THE GREAT UNKNOWN. HE BECAME UPSET. TO THINK OF HOW LITTLE HE'D ACCOMPLISHED, WHEN COMPARED TO THIS GREAT MAN! ALEXANDER HAD CONQUERED THE KNOWN WORLD BY AGE THIRTY. CAESAR VOWED TO MAKE SOMETHING OF HIS LIFE WHEN HE RETURNED TO ROME.

Soon, Caesar's name was on everyone's tongue. From one end of the Republic to the other, he had made friends and gained their support. He was well on his way to the very top of Roman politics.

Chapter 6
Landing the Big Jobs

Ten years after being elected pontifex, Caesar ran for *pontifex maximus*—the highest priesthood in Rome. He was up against two older and more experienced men.

Already deep in debt from running the games, Caesar borrowed more money to get elected. Crassus was among Caesar's most generous supporters. He was one of the richest men in Rome.

CRASSUS

Caesar was risking everything. If he lost, he'd never gain the power and influence necessary to make the money back. He would have to flee the city, with angry creditors on his tail! As he left home the day of the big vote, Caesar told his mother he'd return either "as pontifex maximus . . . or as a fugitive."

But of course, the people's choice was Julius Caesar!

The new position came with a new house. After thirty-seven years in Subura, Caesar moved his family into their beautiful new home right in the center of town.

Two years later, the Senate appointed Caesar to be governor of Spain. As governor, Caesar could collect taxes and steal from rebellious cities. Caesar still owed a lot of money.

In Spain, Caesar's armies crushed local tribes who had been troublesome to Rome. He also got the province's finances in order (taking some silver for himself while he was at it). Soon, Caesar had almost enough money to repay his loans. But even better for the Republic, he had brought peace to Spain for the first time in decades.

BIBULUS

Now certainly was the moment for Caesar to reach for even more power. So he ran for consul. When the votes were counted, Caesar came in first, and a man named Bibulus came in second.

They became co-consuls for the year 59 BC.

Bibulus did not share Caesar's beliefs. He and his allies in the Senate did everything they could to keep Caesar from succeeding.

Caesar needed powerful friends of his own. He always counted on Crassus. Now he looked to a popular general named Pompey. Crassus and Pompey did not like each other, but Caesar thought all three men could help one another out. They formed a secret alliance. To seal this alliance,

POMPEY

Caesar gave his daughter in marriage to Pompey.

Recently, Pompey's armies had defeated pirates and conquered new lands in the Middle East. This made Rome very rich. Pompey wanted to reward some of his hardworking troops with land. For years, the Senate refused to grant his wish. But now, as consul, Caesar came up with a law that gave land to some soldiers as well as Rome's urban poor. Most said it was a good and fair plan.

With taxes from Rome's newest territories, it wouldn't cost the Republic a cent. But Caesar's enemies in the Senate, as well as his co-consul, Bibulus, refused to hold a vote.

Caesar took it to the people. In front of a large crowd, Pompey and Crassus spoke in favor of the law. The people roared their approval.

Bibulus was furious at the thought of his own power slipping away.

Caesar begged Bibulus to listen to the crowd and support the law. People were angry at Bibulus.

They threw things at him. Someone dumped a basket of animal poop on his head, and a mob chased him back to his house. Bibulus hid there, humiliated, for the rest of the year. Now Caesar was the only consul in power.

After their year in office, consuls were given a new job by the Senate. Pompey and Crassus helped secure Caesar a post as governor . . . of *three* of Rome's northern provinces! For five years, he would rule over a territory that stretched from southern France to Macedonia. This was great news for Caesar—as governor he could once again collect taxes and become rich. But his sights were set higher, beyond his provinces' borders—to a vast, unconquered land called Gaul.

GALLIA TRANSALPINA

GALLIA CISALPINA

ILLYRICUM

CAESAR'S TERRITORIES AS GOVERNOR

The warlike tribes of Gaul—and their fearsome neighbors, the Germans—frightened the Romans. If Caesar brought Gaul under Rome's control, he would be a hero! A hero like Alexander the Great.

In 58 BC, Caesar left home again and traveled north. He was forty-one years old. He would not return to Rome until after his fiftieth birthday.

Chapter 7
The Conquest of Gaul

Gaul encompassed modern-day France, Belgium, northern Italy, and parts of Switzerland, Holland, and Germany. Two areas of Gaul had been conquered and settled into two Roman provinces before Caesar was born. It was from these lands that Caesar would raise armies to conquer the rest of Gaul.

The fighting in Gaul began with a tribe from the Swiss Alps. They wanted to move from the mountains to the Atlantic coast, where there was more land for farming. They also wished to be far away from their violent German neighbors. The tribe had planned this move for years. Unfortunately, they had to cross the Rhône River, into Roman territory, to get where they wanted to go.

Caesar rushed with his army to confront the tribe in the town of Geneva. Tribal ambassadors insisted they meant no harm to Rome. They only wanted safe passage to the coast. But Caesar wasn't taking any chances. Three hundred thousand Gauls were on the move, and they had burned their villages behind them, so no one could change their mind and move back home.

Caesar was tricky. He told the ambassadors he would consider their request. He told them to return in two weeks for his answer. All this was a lie.

Once they left, Caesar destroyed the bridge across the Rhône. Then he built a sixteen-foot wall that followed the river for nineteen miles!

When the tribe returned, they were shocked to find their route blocked! Those who tried to cross on foot or by boat were easy targets for the Roman archers. The survivors had no choice but to go back to their burned-out homeland in the mountains.

As word of this defeat spread, some tribes in Gaul pledged loyalty to Caesar. Others fought against him. But one by one, the tribes fell.

Caesar inspired fierce loyalty in his troops. He fought bravely alongside them in battle. He called each man "comrade" rather than "soldier" and knew many by name.

Roman soldiers were well equipped in battle. They wore flexible chain-mail suits made of bronze or iron. They wore sturdy leather sandals with studs on the soles to prevent wear and tear during long marches. They had many weapons.

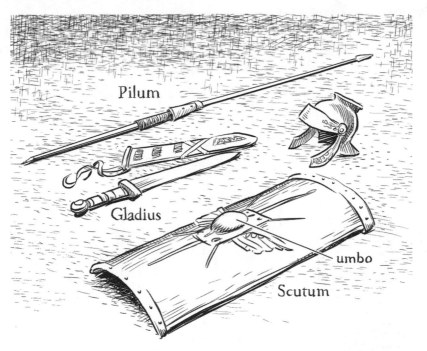

Pilum

Gladius

umbo

Scutum

A six-foot-long spear was called a *pilum*. The
gladius, or short sword, was double-edged, very
sharp, and just under two feet long. It was used
for quick stabs and slashes at close range. A
lightweight shield called a *scutum* measured up to
four feet tall and about two feet across. It curved
at the sides for better protection and had a metal
boss—or *umbo*—in its center that was perfect for
punching an opponent in hand-to-hand combat.

Caesar's troops were often outnumbered, but their skills won out. If an enemy took refuge inside walled cities, Caesar's men built moveable siege towers that could be wheeled right up to the city walls.

Once, Caesar built a bridge across the Rhine River *just* to punish a Germanic tribe. The Germans had been raiding a tribe on the Gaulish side of the river—a tribe that was loyal to Rome. Caesar ordered his men to build a bridge across the river. At the time, it was the longest bridge in the world, and it was built in just ten days! The Roman troops crossed the Rhine and taught the Germans never to mess with a friend of Rome. After crossing the bridge back into Gaul, Caesar ordered it to be torn down. He had proven his point!

COMMENTARIES ON THE GALLIC WAR

EACH YEAR, CAESAR SENT A REPORT TO THE SENATE DETAILING HIS ACTIONS IN GAUL. THESE WERE LATER GATHERED INTO A BOOK CALLED *COMMENTARIES ON THE GALLIC WAR*.

CAESAR WAS AS GOOD A WRITER AS HE WAS AN ORATOR AND GENERAL. HIS ACCOUNTS WERE SIMPLE YET EXCITING, AND HIS WORDS WERE READ ALOUD IN THE FORUM. IT WAS GOOD PUBLICITY FOR CAESAR DURING HIS LONG ABSENCE FROM HOME.

WHEN PEOPLE HEARD HIS ACCOUNTS OF
BATTLING THE GERMANS, THEY MUST HAVE BEEN
AMAZED—NO ROMAN ARMY HAD EVER CROSSED
THE RHINE RIVER.

CAESAR ALSO SAILED TO BRITAIN TWICE.
THERE HE ENCOUNTERED FIERCE WARRIORS ON
CHARIOTS. MANY OF HIS TROOPS WERE KILLED.
THE BATTLES WERE UNSUCCESSFUL. BUT PEOPLE
IN ROME WERE SO IMPRESSED WITH CAESAR'S
BRAVE ADVENTURES THAT TWENTY DAYS OF
CELEBRATIONS WERE HELD IN HIS HONOR.

As his first five-year term as governor drew to a close, Caesar returned to northern Italy to meet with Crassus and Pompey. Caesar wanted to stay in Gaul for another five years. His allies agreed to get themselves elected as co-consuls to make it happen.

Back in Gaul, Caesar met his most capable foe in 53 BC. His name was Vercingetorix, and he united dozens of Gaulish tribes to fight the Romans. He convinced the Gauls to burn their towns and crops and flee to walled cities for protection. Vercingetorix planned to starve Caesar's army into surrendering. The plan caught the Romans by surprise. But Caesar would never give up.

Eventually, Caesar's troops cornered Vercingetorix and his men in Alesia. Quickly Caesar surrounded the walled city with another wall. He

VERCINGETORIX

booby-trapped the ground between the two walls by digging pits and burying sharp stakes in the dirt.

Roman archers stood guard all along Caesar's wall. The people of Alesia were trapped in their city. They began to starve. More tribesmen were on their way to help Vercingetorix. To guard

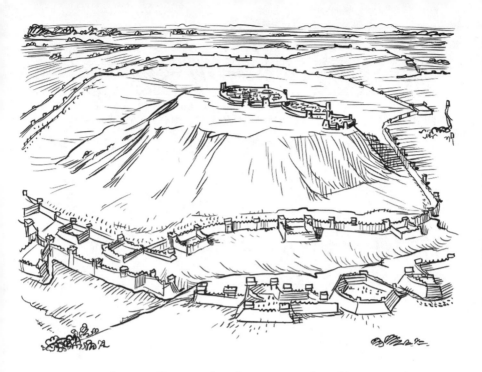

against them, Caesar built a *second* wall around
the first wall he'd built.

When the Gaulish reinforcements arrived,
the Romans were ready. The final battle was
fierce. The Romans repelled attacks from both
directions—Caesar even lost his sword!—but in
the end, Vercingetorix surrendered. Caesar sold
everyone into slavery and arrested their leader.
Vercingetorix was thrown in prison in Rome.

More battles would be fought, but the siege of
Alesia was the Gauls' last real chance to hold back
Caesar. From then on, he could not be stopped.
By 50 BC, Caesar had conquered all of Gaul.

Chapter 8
Civil War

After ten years in Gaul, it was time to return home. Caesar, now one of the richest and most popular men in Rome, hoped to rule again as consul. But he still had many enemies. Some wanted to put him on trial for things he'd done as consul. The Senate sent word to Caesar, ordering him to dismiss his army before returning home.

To make matters worse, Caesar no longer had his alliance to help him. Crassus was dead. Pompey had grown jealous of Caesar's popularity. And Pompey's wife—Caesar's daughter, Julia—had just died in childbirth. Both Caesar and Pompey were grief-stricken. But their relationship did not grow stronger from this loss. When Caesar offered Pompey another chance to join their families in marriage, Pompey refused. Instead he married the daughter of one of Caesar's rivals.

Unsure of his next move, Caesar set up camp with his troops along the Rubicon, the stream that separated Italy from Gaul. When he was ordered again to abandon his troops, Caesar told the Senate he would gladly comply . . . if Pompey did the same. Pompey had large armies of his own, but they were in faraway Spain.

Caesar had a difficult choice to make. If he defied the Senate and kept his army, he would become an enemy of the state. If he obeyed, he knew he'd be arrested for other crimes the moment he entered Rome without protection. And if he took too long to decide, Pompey could summon his troops from Spain in time to attack Caesar.

In the end, Caesar—ever the daring soldier—chose to march. On the morning of January 10, 49 BC, he led his troops across the Rubicon, crying out: "The die is cast!"

Taken by surprise, Pompey and his supporters in the Senate fled south from Rome. He was able to gather some troops and supplies along the way. But his large army was still hundreds of miles away in Spain. Caesar followed close behind Pompey.

Cities threw open their gates to welcome their conquering hero, and Caesar added more troops.

Even so, Caesar wanted to avoid another civil war. He sent messengers to Pompey requesting a meeting. Pompey, however, refused to meet.

Pompey escaped to Greece and began raising an army to take on Caesar and his men.

Caesar returned to Rome, where he seized gold and silver from the treasury to fund the war.

In the fall, almost one year after crossing the Rubicon, Caesar led his army to Greece. Unfortunately, he discovered he was greatly outnumbered! For eight months, Pompey's army blocked the coastline, trying to defeat Caesar's exhausted troops by starvation.

Against all odds, Caesar finally defeated Pompey's army.

Pompey disguised himself as a peasant and fled. But Caesar followed him all the way to Alexandria, in Egypt.

Egypt, too, was in the middle of its own civil war. Ptolemy XIII, the teenage king, was in a power struggle with his sister, twenty-one-year-old Queen Cleopatra. Ptolemy (TALL-uh-mee) and his advisers had kicked Cleopatra out of the royal

PTOLEMY XIII

palace. She was raising an army of her own to fight for the throne.

CLEOPATRA

Ptolemy needed Caesar's support in his fight against Cleopatra. He had heard of Caesar's victory over Pompey and wanted to get on the winner's good side. So his advisers presented Caesar with a welcome gift upon his arrival: a woven basket . . . containing Pompey's severed head!

Julius Caesar's bitter rival, once his close ally and son-in-law, was dead.

Chapter 9
"I Came. I Saw. I Conquered."

Caesar was not pleased by the king's gruesome offering. He was angry. Caesar stormed Ptolemy's palace, trapping the king inside. This angered the residents of Alexandria. Egypt was independent—how dare a Roman general hold their leader

prisoner inside his own palace! Deadly riots broke
out. But Caesar wouldn't leave until Egypt's
civil war was settled. A kingdom as wealthy and
powerful as Egypt could be dangerous to Rome if
it remained unstable.

Caesar wished to settle the king and queen's
differences quickly. He sent for Cleopatra, but
Ptolemy's guards stopped her from meeting the
Roman ruler. So one night, Cleopatra devised
a plan. She had a servant deliver her to Caesar's
room—wrapped up in a rug! Caesar was so
impressed with her cleverness, some say he fell in
love with her immediately.

Many Egyptians loved Cleopatra, too. Caesar realized that Cleopatra was the better choice to rule the kingdom. Caesar summoned Ptolemy. The young king was surprised to find his sister sitting next to Caesar—and in his own palace! When he realized that Caesar was taking Cleopatra's side, he ran to the crowd gathered outside, threw off his crown, and cried! Caesar assured the Egyptians that his intentions were pure. All he wanted was peace for Egypt. He proposed that brother and sister rule together.

Meanwhile, Ptolemy's troops were closing in.
The Egyptian navy attacked Caesar's ships in
the harbor. City residents watched the dramatic
naval battles from the rooftops. Egyptians from all
over poured into Alexandria to fight the Romans.
Caesar's troops fought from house to house in the
city streets surrounding the palace. This was not
the type of battle Caesar was used to fighting, but
he held off the Egyptians.

Eventually, ships loaded with soldiers for
Caesar's army arrived on the Nile River. Egyptian
forces moved to the same area of the Nile.

In the battle that followed, Caesar was victorious and Ptolemy drowned. Caesar returned to Alexandria to name Cleopatra queen of Egypt.

Caesar had been in Egypt for months. He'd been at war for a decade. It was time for a vacation! So he and Cleopatra took a leisurely monthlong cruise down the Nile. But even vacation had a purpose for Caesar. Four hundred Roman ships sailed with them. This sent a clear message to the people of Egypt: Mess with your queen, and suffer at the hands of Caesar.

Before Caesar left Egypt, Cleopatra gave birth to a baby boy, Caesar's only son. She named him Ptolemy XV, but the Egyptians called him Caesarion, or "Little Caesar."

Caesar traveled through the Middle East on his way back to Rome, settling disputes, collecting payments, and putting down rebellions in the provinces along the way. After squashing one rebellion, he uttered a phrase that would become forever famous: *"Veni. Vidi. Vici."* I came. I saw. I conquered.

Once back in Rome, Caesar could finally repay his troops for their years of loyal service. They were given handsome bonuses, and provided with land all around the Republic. Caesar also appointed some of his old soldiers and tribal allies to the Senate.

Lavish parades were organized for Caesar's homecoming. The Romans were amazed by the mountains of treasure and exotic animals from Caesar's conquests. No one in Rome had ever seen a giraffe before!

His great enemy in Gaul, Vercingetorix, was taken
out of jail and paraded through the streets with
other prisoners of war before being executed.

Following Roman tradition, a slave whispered
into Caesar's ear during the celebrations.

"Remember, you are mortal," he told the great ruler. Despite this, Caesar probably felt like a god after all he'd accomplished. He declared himself dictator for ten more years. Consuls would still be elected, but Caesar would always speak first in the Senate meetings. And his word was law.

It seemed that nothing could stop Julius Caesar.

The dictator left Rome one last time to defeat Pompey's remaining supporters in Spain. With the help of

OCTAVIUS

his grand-nephew, Octavius, he was successful. He held another celebration upon his return. But this parade did not impress Romans. Caesar's other wars had seemed justified; now it seemed like he was just slaughtering fellow Romans.

The Senate—probably terrified of him—
gave Caesar a throne made of solid gold.

The month of *Quinctilus* was officially renamed
in his honor: *Julius*, or July. Caesar's birthday was
proclaimed a public holiday for all time.

And he was named dictator . . . *for life*!

Julius Caesar once said: "The Republic is
nothing. Just a name without substance or form."
It appeared now that the Roman Republic—
almost five hundred years after its birth—was
truly dying.

Chapter 10
The Ides of March

The dictator did much good for the Republic. He put Romans to work digging ports and canals, and made plans to build a grand library. He granted citizenship—and all the rights that came with it—to many living in the provinces.

New colonies were established in far-flung reaches of the Republic, and Caesar sent eighty thousand Romans to start new lives there. He also started a project to record all of Rome's laws in one place—a process that would take hundreds of years.

But Caesar's love of power also made Romans nervous and fearful. He had coins minted with his image. He placed a statue of himself among statues of the gods. He put one of Cleopatra in the Temple of Venus. Some feared he would take Cleopatra as his queen and rule over Rome from Egypt . . . as a *king*!

After all, he had taken to wearing the traditional purple toga of the ancient kings.

In early 44 BC, a group of senators met in secret to discuss what to do about Caesar. They called themselves "the liberators." Marcus Brutus, a man whom Caesar had known since Brutus was a baby, was among them.

MARCUS BRUTUS

The liberators decided the only way to save the Republic was to murder its dictator.

Early one morning, Caesar's wife, Calpurnia, awoke from a terrible nightmare. In it, she was holding her husband's lifeless body. It was March 15, the Ides of March. Days earlier, Caesar had been warned by a fortune-teller that something terrible would happen on this day. Caesar's wife begged him to stay home, but Caesar refused.

As Caesar walked through the Forum, he was
approached by a man who worked for Brutus. The
man had heard about the plan to murder Caesar.
Afraid to speak aloud, the man slipped Caesar a
scroll of paper explaining everything. But Caesar
was in a hurry and merely put the scroll with some
other papers he was carrying.

Next, Caesar saw the fortune-teller. He laughed and told her she had been wrong—it was the Ides of March, and he was alive and well! The fortune-teller cautioned Caesar that the day was not over yet.

Upon Caesar's arrival in the Senate hall, a group of men surrounded him. One senator whose brother had been exiled by Caesar asked him for a pardon. When Caesar refused, the man tugged on Caesar's toga, begging him for mercy.

This was the signal.

The first to stab Caesar was a senator named Casca. He was so nervous that he only grazed Caesar's neck. Caesar attacked with the only weapon he had—a pen—and stabbed it through Casca's arm. Twenty-two more blows descended on Caesar, one knife after another. Could this really be how the great commander would die?

Caesar fought for his life, wildly, until he saw Marcus Brutus. The boy he had known and mentored for so many years raised his weapon to strike.

"Even you, my child?" a shocked Julius Caesar said as the knife came down.

Refusing to let his enemies see him die, Caesar pulled his toga over his head and collapsed dead on the Senate floor. He was fifty-five years old.

Rome erupted into chaos. Fearing for their lives, Caesar's allies fled the city. After Caesar's death, the fight to control Rome raged for more than a decade. Caesar's heir, Octavius, defeated his uncle's enemies, ending the Republic—and open debate and free elections—forever.

In its place rose the Roman Empire. At its height, it stretched from Scotland to Egypt, connecting the world as never before. Octavius became Rome's first emperor, changing his name to Caesar Augustus and ruling as supreme leader.

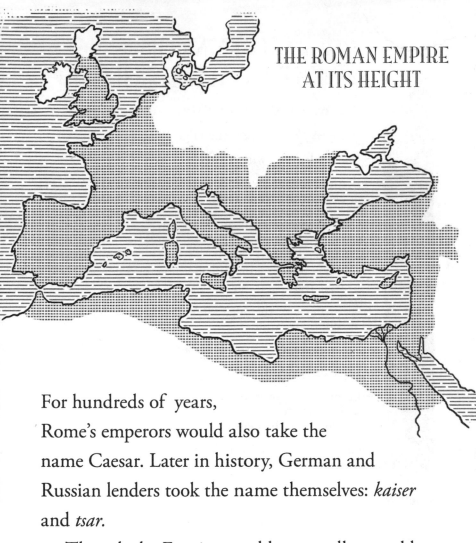

THE ROMAN EMPIRE
AT ITS HEIGHT

For hundreds of years,
Rome's emperors would also take the
name Caesar. Later in history, German and
Russian lenders took the name themselves: *kaiser*
and *tsar*.

Though the Empire would eventually crumble,
Julius Caesar's name remains eternal.

TIMELINE OF
JULIUS CAESAR'S LIFE

100 BC — Born on July 13

87 BC — Becomes *flamen dialis*, the High Priest of Jupiter

84 BC — Marries his first wife, Cornelia

80 BC — Battles Mithridates in Asia, and is awarded the *corona civica*, or civic crown, for bravery

75 BC — Captured by Cilician pirates

77 BC — Becomes an advocate in Rome

69 BC — Cornelia and his aunt Julia both die
Elected as *quaestor*, and moves to Spain

63 BC — Campaigns for the position of *pontifex maximus* of Rome, and wins

61 BC — Appointed the governor of Spain

59 BC — Elected as consul of Rome

58 BC — Becomes the governor of Transalpine Gaul, Cisalpine Gaul, and Illyricum
Beginning of the Gaulish Wars

55 BC — Crosses the Rhine into Germany
Becomes first Roman general to travel to Britain

52 BC — Defeats Vercingetorix at Alesia

49 BC — Crosses the Rubicon, setting off a civil war

48 BC — Defeats Pompey's forces in Greece
Travels to Egypt and meets Cleopatra

47 BC — Defeats the army of Ptolemy XIII and names Cleopatra queen

44 BC — Becomes dictator for life
Stabbed to death on March 15, the Ides of March

TIMELINE OF
THE WORLD

Ironworking is brought to East Africa — **CA. 100 BC**
by the Bantu people
In the American Southwest, the Ancient Pueblo people
start building underground "pit houses"

The cities of Italy revolt against Rome, — **91 BC**
beginning the Social War

Sulla ends the Social War — **88 BC**
First Roman civil war between Sulla and Marius

Emperor Wu dies after ruling China — **87 BC**
for a record fifty-four years

End of Sulla's second civil war in Rome — **81 BC**
Sulla appointed dictator

Spartacus leads a slave revolt in southern Italy — **73-71 BC**

The Roman poet Virgil is born — **70 BC**

Pompey defeats the Mediterranean pirates — **67 BC**

Syria becomes a province of the Roman Republic — **64 BC**

Jerusalem falls to Pompey's army — **63 BC**

The Kingdom of Xiongnu, in modern-day — **60 BC**
Mongolia, breaks out in civil war

Silla, one of the Three Kingdoms of Korea, is founded — **57 BC**

Cleopatra and Ptolemy XIII become joint — **51 BC**
rulers of Egypt

Glass-blowing techniques invented by the Phoenicians — **CA. 50 BC**

Egypt becomes part of the Roman Empire — **30 BC**

BIBLIOGRAPHY

Caesar, Julius. **The Battle for Gaul: A New Illustrated Translation**. Translated by Anne and Peter Wiseman. Boston: David R. Godine, Publisher, 1980.

Freeman, Philip. **Julius Caesar**. London: JR Books, 2008.

Goldsworthy, Adrian. **Caesar: Life of a Colossus**. New Haven and London: Yale University Press, 2006.

Holland, Tom. **Rubicon: The Last Years of the Roman Republic**. New York: Anchor Books, 2005.

* Rinaldo, Denise. **Julius Caesar: Dictator for Life**. New York: Franklin Watts, 2010.

* Books for young readers